# Contents

## "My Poetry"

This doggerel is what I pass off for verse.
It's the best I can do, it could be even worse!
There's no fancy structure, or big long words
Sometimes it rhymes
And sometimes it don't!
The grammar and spelling and balance are often wrong too
But it's the best this simple country lad can do.
Ignore the mistakes and the crass simplicity,
There's a message within, if you could just see!

## Planet Syd

Welcome to Planet Syd
Home of a far out kid.
Where things are groovy and cool.
The sun shines and there aint no pain.
You only get night time rain
And we don't bother with any rules.
Welcome to Planet Syd
I'm afraid you can't come in.
Because you're just a worn out old has been.
You're boring and you're straight laced
 And oh so middle class.
Which in Syd speak means
You're just a pain in the arse.
Folk say I'm a freak and they diss  me with bad vibes.
They say I'm somewhere else, but hell I'm still alive
They don't understand my cosmic speak
And think I'm really weird.
In my mind I'm on my planet
Supping ice cold beer.

## A Plea

Try to walk softly upon this land,
Go with nature hand in hand.
Treat this earth with great respect
It is your legacy to those who come next.
Damage you must inevitably sometimes do
But balance it with repairs and renew
The fabric whenever you can
Restore the ravages of man.

# The Woodcutter's Lament

I'm a woodcutter and folk say I'm no good
But Jesus was a carpenter, and he too, worked with wood.
He knew all about knots, and bonny straight grain
And also about callouses and slipped tools causing pain.
I reckon we could have good craic about our lives with timber
But before that happens, there is something that hinders
My burden of sin, my passport to Hell,
Self destruction is my aim, I know it all too well.
For I cut the timber that was used at Calvary
The wood that was stained, like my soul, upon that bloody day.
It wasn't personal, it was just another job.
Have mercy on me Lord, Jesus, Son of God.

# The Loner

When I work in the wood
I prefer to be on "my tod;"
No one sees my fear or anxiety
Grafting away among the trees
The successes, failures or stupidity
It's all just for me to see.
Responsible for no one except me,
No distractions, no worries, a conscience free.
No guilt for harming someone else's son,
Husband, partner, friend or loved one.
The snapping rope, the swinging tree
The shattered limbs, the misery.
If there's to be blood on the forest floor I'd rather it was my own.
If someone has to walk down the Valley of Death, I'd prefer it was
me alone.

## Hillbilly rebel

People laugh at the clothes I wear,
People laugh at the sawdust in my hair.
They think I'm dumb and stupid you see.
But I don't give a damn. I'm just little old me.
I'm a hillbilly rebel from head to toe
Creating mayhem wherever I go.
Come and join me, keep some bad company
And be a real kool kat, be a hillbilly rebel like me.
Folk go east and I go west
I sure am different from all the rest.
Being in trouble since the age of three,
I just don't get on with authority.
I pay little tax or V.A.T.
Rules and regulations are a mystery to me.
Stuff the paperwork and bureaucracy
Cos I just like to be free and easy.

# The Middle Class Nyaff Song

We're a persecuted bunch in this Strath,
Surrounded by a bunch of middle class nyaffs.
I don't give a hoot, I don't give a damn.
I'm going to take a rebel stand.
The middle class nyaffs moved out from town
They call us locals a bunch of dumb clowns.
They think they're superior, they treat us like dirt
Just 'cos we make our living from the earth.
The middle class nyaffs hate me cutting down trees
And they don't like the smell of manure on the breeze.
Whatever we do they say it's wrong.
I bet they don't even like this song.
I'm going to drive my tractor slow down the strath
Just to annoy those middle class nyaffs
I'll run them off the road and into a ditch
They'll call me a mean son-of-a-bitch.

# The Chain Saw

The chain saw is a fearsome tool,
Like the broadswords of old.
It can lay low both the mighty and the weak
Treating neither with respect.
And yet the cross cut had its strengths.
No fumes, no oil spewing out
Fouling the pure, clear air.
Little noise, so you could still hear
The birdsong and the creaks
And shudders of the tree
As it gave ready to give up the ghost,
To fall, shattering, to the ground.
You had extra, vital seconds
To step aside, to safety.
The chainsaw is kingmaker now,
A deadly weapon in the hands of a warrior.
Yet disfigurement or death lie but a heartbeat away.
For this weapon cuts not only wood but living tissue too,
Nerves, sinews, bone and muscle
To make a mistake, could be fatal.
Trees can swing round, to catch the unwary.
Like a warrior before battle
As I prepare to fell a mighty tree I feel apprehensive and pray
Lord, if I should forget thee today
Please do not thou forget me.

8

## Guitars and Chainsaws

I'm just an old fashioned lad, a relic from a by-gone age.
Just a dinosaur lost in time.
Don't do things electronic, don't do things digital.
I'm just a hillbilly, wood cutting boy.
*The world is changing fast around me.*
*Sometimes I feel adrift and lonely,*
*But guitars and chain saws make me smile*
Don't do things touchy feely, don't do political correctness.
I speak my mind and get myself in trouble.
Can't keep to the straight and narrow, push things to the limit.
Always seem to be out of step.
*The world is changing fast around me.*
*Sometimes I feel adrift and lonely,*
*But guitars and chain saws make me smile*
I base my life on different values, try to make my character
assessments
On who a person is, not what they're worth.
Judge a man by his deeds and actions, on what he does, not what
he says.
Fancy words cut no ice with me.
*The world is changing fast around me.*
*Sometimes I feel adrift and lonely,*
*But guitars and chain saws make me smile*

## Sawmill Work

I love this orange coloured Canadian bandsaw machine,
Slicing through the wood, leaving edges clean.
Working through the lumber pile making boards, rails and planks
Turning out the timber to make sheds, gates and fanks
From 6" to 31"logs and everything in between
Open up the throttle and hear the blade scream.
Whatever your requirements, watch the sawdust fly
And stack the finished timber up to the sky.
Smell the resin and marvel at the sawyer's skill
As he converts a pile of sticks into something really useful.

# The Old Birch Tree

I'm going to cut down a big birch tree
To keep us warm when it gets frosty.
My wife is getting on and growing old.
When winter comes she feels the cold.
I'm sorry tree, you must pay the price. The ultimate sacrifice.
On my poor wages I just can't pay
The prices the fuel companies want today.
I did the deed, I cut her down.
Saw her fall to the mossy ground.
Now my conscience bothers me.
Over the death of that old tree.
Logged and split and stacked her at home.
Seasoned till as dry as a bone.
On the fire all winter long.
The heat she gave was mighty strong.
Sitting cosy, one winter's night
Gazing at the bright fire light.
News was coming from out of the hearth.
I swear it was the voice of Mother Earth.
So I decided to absolve my sins,
And got me some fine saplings.
Planted them little 'uns one, two, three
Round the base of that old tree.
Protected them all with netting wire,
Watched them grow higher and higher.
Now my conscience lets me sleep,
And Mother Earth no longer weeps.

# The Old Larch

She has stood for well over a hundred years, until the lightening
bolt hit her.
Hacked fifteen feet off her crown,
And split the trunk right down the middle, till just three foot from the
ground.
I had to fell her then, for she was no longer safe.
She was difficult to the last.
I cut and cut, hammered in wedges, still she would not yield,
But at last, she gave out her death groan,
To fall, wretchedly, to the ground.
Heavy limbed and branched,
I cut and cut again, so twisted had she grown.
There was scarce a length fit for the mill.
Log after log I cut.
Stacked branches and burnt them.
Then I split the logs.
Everyone was dour, knotted and hard.
They repelled the axe.
So, with metal wedges and sledgehammer,
I hewed and split on frosty days.
Sweat coursing down,
Jersey and shirt cast aside though ground was hard as iron.
I loaded logs onto trailer, stacked them in the shed
The boss claimed them, burnt them on the open fire,
Where, with a final act of defiance
The old lady spat cinders onto the carpet
Like a witch cursing those who burnt her.
I found some young trees, growing in the flower borders.
I transplanted them near her stump.
Time will pass, her stump will rot.
I too will go from this place,
But our legacy, hopefully, will live on.

# First Thinnings

Here I am again, cutting, hacking, felling trees
Whatever the weather, sun, rain, or freeze.
A wood to be thinned-my winter's work
It will be hard going and I cannot shirk.
I'm a one man squad, progress is slow
Lack of time my greatest foe.
Don't look back at how little done
When you start the job when winter's begun.
Nor look forward at so much to do,
Just plod on and see the winter through.
For the season passes and the spring will come
And so the job will be finished and all done.
You'll reach the other side, never fear
And if you don't, there's always another year!

## The Last of a Dying Breed

I  am the last of a dying breed, who works to nature's tune.
Struggling against the elements in a way of life that'll end soon.
I walk most places, striding out my measured pace upon the sod
But the younger generation ride in Land Rover or on 4 wheeled quad.
Tractors now have fancy cabs, with radio and computer
No need to struggle in wind and rain, travelling in comfort is so much cuter.
But I hear the birds, and feel the breeze and sun upon my face.
I know the short cuts through the wood as I walk from place to place.
I know the birds, beasts, flowers and trees; know which way the cold wind comes.
I know where to shelter from the icy blast, and where shines the early morning sun.
Folk laugh at me, call me a fool for my old fashioned ways.
They jeer, and scoff, and mock so cruel
 For they can't see through their own mind's haze

# The Country Man

This way of life is dying fast.
No more the farmers boy walks the fields
To the sound of curlew and peewit.
Now he rides in tractor, pick-up, or A.T.V.
Radio and cassette now do him accompany.
For how can stewardship of the land
Be matched with efficiency?
Cost effectiveness demands
More land, more animals, but fewer hands
So the old ways go
So did I.
Yet when I walk the fields, now for pleasure,
Still, I gather up stones
Carrying them to the dyke,
And still I count the sheep
Though they are no longer any concern of mine.
You can take the man from the country,
But you can never take the country from this man.

# <u>Vindication</u>   *1999*

Why do I do this job?
Enduring nature's worst,
Pay that is not a muckle cop,
And low esteem from my fellow man.
The nice things in life pass me by,
Beyond my financial reach.
And yet I am so rich in other ways.
This job is worth it, I convince myself.
For if I do not care for the countryside, who else will?
In an age when so many want to take,
And put nothing back.
"Let it go wild," some say.
Wilderness!  Have you ever lived in it?
Struggled through shoulder high bracken,
Or heather up to your knees,
Sunk in bogs
Or seen the dereliction of tumbledown dykes and crofts?
The best landscapes are where man and nature work hand in
hand,
Each complementing the other.
We have lost so much.
Concrete and tarmac spread on and on.
Where will our grand children play?
Or ourselves, when our day's work is done?
This job is worth it and must be done.
And if I am the one to bear the yoke
That is the burden I must carry on.

## Working on the Land

There used to be a big squad working round here,
Toiling away on the land, throughout the year.
Now they've gone and I'm left to work away, alone.
There used to be a big squad working round here
It's a lonely life working the land all the day.
Farmers, shepherds, foresters have now all left or gone away.
The houses are full of townie folk who just don't understand
This is not a recreation park but a living land.
Who do you think cares for this land, when you are not around?
When you finish your leisure time, do you think it all goes to sleep?
Put the land back into the toy box for another week.
Who maintains the track you use when you go for a walk?
You say you care for this land, but it's all just empty talk.
I've never seen you pick up litter or put a stone back in the dyke.
Our right to earn a living takes second place to your access rights.

# Winter on the Land *1999*

Despite all our new technology,
Winter on the land is still a hard place to be.
Cold and damp assault your bones.
Fingers and toes ache, the body groans
Under the attack of rain, hail and snow
All pervading damp and the winds blow.
Wellies, coat and leggings which seemed so light
When first were donned at break of day
Weigh heavy as chains by darkening night.
Soaked with wet and clarted with clay.
Simple jobs take twice as long
When imprisoned in waterproofs, with fingers numb.
All nature suffers with you in this terrible time
Plants, birds, animals, sheep and kine.
Yesterday I found a young roe
Struck down by hunger, awaiting death's blow.
Feebly kicking, streaked out on the ground
Death would not come, till I came around
I smashed in it's skull, gave it release.
Some say I am cruel, but I brought it peace
For death is not always quick and without pain
It often lingers, teasing as it maims.
A true countryman knows what to do
To end suffering fast, he sometimes seems cruel.
So why endure it, this terrible time
Why not walk away, down the line?
Get a job in an office in the town
With central heating, warmth all around
Because winter on the land, despite its misery
Is the best place on earth for the likes of me.

# Winter

Winter has returned to the land
Reaching out it's chilly hand.
Your bones they will ache and your hands they will crack
Cold, hard, brutal winter is back.
Anyone can work outside in summer time
Or when the weather is dry or fine.
But when days shorten and nights they grow long
That's when a body has got to be strong.
You wake up in the morn and hear the rain on the roof.
Another day clad in water proofs.
Cold, clammy, stiff and sore.
Can your body take anymore?
But it's not all bad, sometimes there is respite,
Clear frosty days bathed in sunlight.
Lifting your spirits until the light fades,
When cold marches back at the end of the day.
You come through it all and finally spring does arrive.
You think you've done well to stay  alive.
But spring, summer, autumn soon go by.
The days grow dark and snow falls from the sky.
Winter has returned to the land
Reaching out it's chilly hand.
Your bones they will ache and your hands they will crack
Cold, hard, brutal winter is back.

## Shortening Days

The clock went back this Saturday night
From here to February we'll suffer from lack of light.
It's not the cold that greatly bothers me,
But boggling around in the dark which is such drudgery.
Can't see the dog on early morning walks
Tripping over obstacles leaves me out of sorts.
Pressure at work to get things done
Before light fails with setting sun.
There is no neon arc light in field or wood
Except tractor head lights, and they're not much good.
But all is not gloom and dismay,
There'll be a few bonny dawns at break of day
And rosy skies too in late afternoon
As days end, sometimes all too soon.
Twinkling lights as I wend home,
Welcoming wood smoke to warm cold bones.
Winter, like life, we make it what we will,
Happiness or misery, good or ill.

# **Bonfires**

Wood smoke rising,
Brings back happy memories
Of mother in an old coat,
And me, very young,
Burning garden waste.
Old twigs, prunings,
The autumn clear up.
And later, bonfire night
When we would spend an afternoon
Dragging driftwood off Formby beach,
Loading it into the car
And bringing it home,
To stack until the magic night
Of flames and sparklers,
Rockets, whizz-bangs and Catherine wheels.
But, if truth be told,
I liked the bonfire best,
The glow, the heat,
Hot soup, baked tatties and chestnuts.
Now, I still have bonfires
Hag, old branches, rhododendrons go up in flames.
Smoke rising in the winter air,
A grand job for a cold day.

## Passing of time

The year has passed so quickly, the time has flown so fast,
The summer was a damp  squib, the good weather didn't last.
The short days are upon us, and the weather's closed right in.
I could do with some comfort now against the bitter wind.
The warmth of a lover's touch on a cold winter's night.
An easy chair, a faithful dog and the bright firelight.
A glass of whisky, or maybe a pleasant red wine.
As we battern down the hatches against the winter time.
Christmas is coming with the speed of an express train,
For some it's been a good year, but for others filled with pain.
Profit or loss, good health or disease.
Amidst life's turmoil, we search for inner peace.

## Bad Weather Blues

Sometimes in winter especially, when the weather is rough,
I sit at piece time and wish the day was through,
Muscles aching, hands hurt and sore; cold and damp chill my bones.
And I wish I was by the fire with you at home.
Or, later, curled up in bed, cuddled in close
To your curvaceous body, warm as toast
Until then, I must take the strain
Once more struggle on, in the rain.

## December Morn  (in a wood)

The winter dawn it comes so slow,
Sometimes with mirk, and sometimes with rosy glow.
And here in the wood it comes last of all,
To banish the shadows from the forest floor.
Filtering so gently through the trees
Subtlely setting the morning free.
Light so precious I must not waste,
Days so short I must make haste.
Darkness will come to reclaim all
As the light retreats and night falls

# February

This is the low part of the year,
Christmas long gone and Easter nowhere near.
The daylight hours are lengthening,
Yet the cold seems to be strengthening
Cutting right through to the bone
Making me wish I was by the fire at home.
A deceptive month, full of guile.
Last week was so bonny, even mild.
But now winter has swept down again from the hills
Like a ravishing wolf, full of ill will.
Snow, ice, frost, mud, cold, rain
Covers the land, a land filled with the pain
Of longing for spring and warm, mild days
Oh how I wish winter was away
But spring is aye late in these northern lands
And so I must thole  it as best I can

## The Gale

You came in the night, thundering down the strath
Like Ghengis Khan and his Mongal hordes
Laying low the old, the weak and the unprepared.
Only the strong could withstand your hammering blows.
I lay cowering in bed, anxious, frightened and worried
For what devastation I would find in the morning light.
Daylight came and I ventured forth, keeping as much
as I could to shelter.
But, at length, I had to cross bare ground and face
your onslaught head on.
Eyes watering, face numb, head and ears aching, fit to burst.
I clawed my way to the sanctuary of the sawmill.
But even here you made inroads, finding every crack and
 opening. Your chill grip, still, would not let me go.
In the woods, the trees shook and trembled like stampeding
horses.
Branches, twigs, leaves cast everywhere
Onto roads, paths, gutters, the choking debris fell.
Here and there you uprooted whole trees, or snapped them off
like matchsticks.
Proud sentinels, whose form and beauty I had long admired.
 Now cast down upon the ground.
No more would their lofty towers cast shade and provide life and
shelter,
 For bird, insect and animal.
And yet you did me a favour
For every year, some trees must fall to my woodsman's blow
You have saved me from making the fateful decision
Which of my leafy friends must fall, for log and post and rail.
By evening you have gone
Only the odd, straggling gust trailed in your wake.
Peace returned once more.

26

# Frosty Weather

I love the winter when the days are dry,
It banishes depression and lifts my spirits high.
For it sets me free from the tyranny
Of waterproofs clammy misery.
I love the hard, cold, frosty weather
Drying the ground to old, hard, leather
Banishing slime, glaur and mud
Free, for a while, from dirty dubs!
Tomorrow a thaw is due to start,
Oh dear, it's back to grubby clarts!

# Spring's Arrival

Suddenly, spring arrived today.
The jersey was discarded
The weight of winter fell away
As I felt the warm sun caress my back
The best medicine of all.
These are busy days,
The keepers burning on the hill,
The farmers in the fields
Or amongst their flocks and herds.
And me, in the gardens and woods.,
Busy days, and yet
Tiredness slips away.
The step is light,
And spirits soar, like a lark,
On days like these.
These are good days.
Treasure them!

## Good Weather Vibes

A day like this makes up for all the bad times,
The cold, the pain, the mud and grime.
Sit at rest and feel the breeze,
Watch the sunlight filter through the trees.
Listen to the bird song fill the air
Watch the squirrel, roe and hare.
Wild flowers strew all around
With bilberry covering the ground.
No one counting how long I take,
For my extended tea break!
The saw is silent, tractor too,
I've worked hard and paid my dues!
Rest and relax, drink all nature's beauty in
Simon's on the scive again!

## April Morning

A thin mist half covers the land,
Caressing it like a gentle hand.
Through the mist filters the sun's early rays
With the promise of what will be a glorious day.
A touch of frost cools the air,
Birds sing loud and clear.
The woods take on a mystical hue,
You could believe in goblins, elves and fairies too.
This is a land of magic and myth,
Of music, mystery, happiness and grief.
Stand quiet, at peace, feel its power
In this its early, waking hour.

# The Dance of Seasons

"Who will dance with me?" said Nature
When I was but a lad.
"I will," said I, and so began an affair
Which will end , who knows where?
She took me on a fiendish jig called Winter,
Wild as the howling wind and driving snow.
On and on it went,
Till, exhausted, I begin to tire.
Suddenly, her mood began to change.
I caught faint glimpses of another dance,
And she gradually drew me
Into a reel of Spring
It too was quick, as new life burst forth
Into our cold, northern hills.
Again the dance changed its tune
A slow dance of high Summer, a stately Strathspey
As she showed off her jewels of beauty.
And then another dance called Autumn.
Sometimes hectic as the Autumn gales,
Sometime slow and thoughtful.
So the year turned.
"Will you dance with me once more?"
 said natureand I totally, bewitched, replied
"Yes" again, again and again.

# Dancing at the Barn

It's a Monday winters night
And I'm dancing at the Barn
But I'd rather be in my shed, or at the fireside warm.
I've had a hard day in the wood,
I've hurt my back and drawn blood.
Slipped and slithered, I ache and I'm sore.
And now I'm at the dancing and Isla's laying down the law.
"You must do the exercises" as if I haven't had enough,
Bend and stretch and point and all that sadistic stuff.
That's fine if you've been sedentary and sitting in a chair
But I've been grafting all day out in the cold damp air.
And if I skive off, and stay by the fire at home
All the lasses start to bother me, on the bloody phone
Why has Simon not come out to play?
We missed you, we need you, is what they all say.
So I wend my weary way down from the hilly strath,
Through sleat, snow, mist and all of winter's wrath.
Huddled in my corner, for the Barn's a draughty place,
Trying to stifle yawns that stretch my weary face.
And Liz Mackenzie gives me rows for being half asleep,
When numbing tiredness over my body creeps.
Now here's Sandra, she scares me half to death
'Cos she likes to burl and I haven't got the breath!
Some lassies want to dance with me, cos they think I'm good
When the only thing I'm useful for is working in the wood.
It's all a bluff, I really don't have a clue,
Most of the time I just don't know what to do.
Muddle through, guess, pray, use any trick that's known to me
Or rely on reactions, honed by years of dodging fallen trees.
But don't get me wrong, I enjoy it despite starting bruised and
battered,
And I'd enjoy it even  more if I wasn't aye BLEEDING SHATTERED.

# Dancing

(dedicated to all the lassies who have helped me)
I'm off to a dance and I feel ill,
Shaking and shivering, insides in knots,
Stomach churning, I grip the steering so tight
Tension rising, I want to take to flight.
With increasing panic, I realise I've forgotten the steps,
Minds gone blank, what a mess!
Now I'm here and into the hall I go,
Footsteps dragging ever so slow.
But you are there and your warm smile
And genuine welcome make it all worthwhile.
The evening begins, I take a deep breath
Ask you to dance and from the depths
Of my memory, come back the moves.
We get through the first dance without too many boobs.
The evening gets better, I relax
Wonder why I had such a panic attack.
Then it's all over oh too soon
We smile, say goodnight and leave the room.
I wonder when the next dance will be,
But I couldn't go, if it wasn't for your kindness to me.

## The Eyes of a Child

I saw the sun today,
Glinting through the trees.
Casting dappled light into the forest glade.
And smelt the leaves and needles upon the ground.
Suddenly I went back in time,
And I was looking through my childhood eyes
With senses keen and clear.
I gazed with rapt and innocent wonder
Upon this woodland scene.
Then, like the clouds across the sun,
The vision was gone
And I returned to adult life.
As we grow older, so we believe
We grow wiser.
But age often brings cares and worries,
Cynicism, guilt, envy, greed,
All mask our minds and deeds.
To see the world through the eyes of a child
Is the mark of a true man.

## Song

Here we go across the hill,
Looking for some grouse to kill,
Over burn and over bog,
Through the heather we slog.
All day long we tramp along
Singing this merry song.

## Hands

What do you think when you see hands like these?
All calloused and worn, like the bark on the trees.
What do you think when you see the ingrained dirt?
And the chapped knuckles and fingers that sting and hurt.
Does the rough touch of them make you recoil and shiver?
Do they embarrass you and make you quiver?
Do they fill you with pity, or loathing and contempt?
Do you think I'm a beast that from hell has been sent?
To the old parson I apologised for taking communion wine
And for kneeling before the altar with hands like mine.
He smiled, said, "You have the hands of an honest man
And Jesus, the carpenter, he too, will understand."

## Sudan  (June 2004)

The four horseman of the Apocalypse ride through the Sudan,
Trailing in their wake, war, death, pestilence and famine.
While we in the West, barely give a damn
For years now, there's been trouble in the bloody Sudan.
Their bodies are black, and they live far away
And we're far too busy with our work and our play.
If we did care what could we do for this land?
Are prayers any use or wringing our hands?
Our charity does it do any good?
Or is it embezzled by men in black hoods?
But think on this thought, before you turn away
But , for the grace of God, that could be you today

## Good Friday  (1998)

Here I am working in a wood
On a Good Friday afternoon.
I should have asked for time off
And gone to kirk instead.
I'll go to Mass tonight and ask
For God's forgiveness.
Yet in this wood, all around
Are things that remind of Calvary.
Yonder thorn tree with its jaggy spikes
Reminds me of the crown he wore
And how it must have torn his scalp.
Yonder Aspen, will rattle in shame
When it bursts forth and bears leaves again.
For if tradition is to be believed
It made the head stock for the cross.
In the bottom of my coat pocket
Are nails, wedge shaped, old, smiddy made
Such as were used to nail him to the tree.
And I am alone
As he was
Deserted by disciples and friends alike.
So though I am not in your house
Lord, I am thinking of thee.

# <u>Holy Week</u> 1999  Tears for Kosovo

It is Holy week
And we are sending our young men
Off to fight a war in a distant land
The causes of which are hard to understand.
In straths and glens like these
Bombs,  bullets and shells rain down
Houses burnt, livelihoods lost.
Maimings, torture, death, the innocent bear the cost
Of mans continuing inhumanity to his fellow man.
2,000 years have come and gone
We are fast approaching a new millennium,
But we have not advanced at all,
Selfishness, greed, cruelty,
We are a primitive race.
This Holy Week we'll pray for love, peace, and forgiveness too.
How long , O Lord, will it be necessary so to do?

# Josh

Josh, he was a hill billy from up north in Galilee.
Josh, he was a working man, same as you and me.
Josh, he was a rebel who took a rebel stand
So the authorities crucified him, and put nails in his hands.
But Josh he didn't die, he got up again
Still walking to this day, helping his fellow man.
Wherever there is discord, suffering or strife
Josh , he will be there to try and make it right.
When the coloured man was suffering in chains and slavery
Josh, he was there sharing their misery.
He stood along side Wilberforce and John Newton too
Gave them the courage to see their abolition through.
When Martin Luther King proclaimed all men the same.
Josh stood beside him and supported his aims.
And when the evil racist gunned poor Martin down
Josh held his hand as he lay dying on the ground.

## Judas

Judas, why did you sell our Lord so cheap?
You must have realised the harvest that you would reap?
Eternal damnation, was that your fate?
Or were you forgiven and brought to Heaven's gate?
Did you not believe He was the Son of God?
Were all his teachings and miracles so misunderstood?
Was it jealousy, greed or hate
That blinded you, or was it your fate
To be predestined to betray
Our Lord on that fateful day?
But if our Lord was not given up and crucified
He would not have risen from dead and been taken up high.
We would still be in the thrall of death and sin
With no hope of salvation from all our sufferings.
Judas I cannot condemn you, I pity thee
For if it had not been you, it could easily have been me.

# Humility

If you want to learn about humility,
Try cutting down a big tall tree.
Crouched at her base, look up to the top,
See how she soars, up and up.
Feel her strength, her power, her might.
If I make a mistake, I'm in the shite.
For let it be clearly understood
Flesh and blood are no match for falling wood.
I feel small, weak, an insignificant blob,
Now I must start this dreadful job.
Heart is pumping in my ear,
Taste the adrenalin, smell the fear.
Start the saw, start the job.
First I cut out a gob.
Then to the back and start to saw,
Anxiety rising more and more.
Have I got it right, where falls this tree?
Where I want it, or, on top of me?
A shudder, a creak, a sickening groan,
Down she falls towards the loam.
Grateful relief swells in me,
And sorrow too, over such a fine tree.
It's down,  I'm safe, all is well
Today for me , no heaven , or hell.

# Mistakes

We try to get through life as best we can
Child or adult, woman and man
But it is human nature to err and make mistakes
And we sometimes cause pain and make hearts break.
I am not perfect, God only knows
How much sorrow I have caused and so much woe.
I open my mouth and speak before my brain is in gear,
And the distress I cause is hard to bear.
All I can do is beg forgiveness and offer it too
When I am on the receiving end of some other fool.
But those of whom you are especially fond,
It takes more than foolishness to break friendships bond.

# Evening Solitude

Sit quiet by the loch and listen
To the gentle gurgle of the water
The birds evening chorus
And hum of bees.
Feel the gentle caress of the breeze,
Like a lovers touch upon your skin.
Drink down this heady wine of nature's bounty.
For a while forget the stresses of your life,
Relax in quiet solitude and reflect
Let the beauty and solitude of this place
Grant you rest and a quiet nights sleep.

# Evening

Tracery of branches against the sky
Silhouetted beauty as evening draws nigh.
Hills outline stands so stark
Defiant against the gathering dark.
Woodcocks flutter, tawny owls shriek
Column of wood smoke from the lum reeks.
First stars twinkle in the sky
Day is done, night draws nigh

## Carrion Crow

Don't you sit cawing at the top of that tree,
Making mockery of me.
You know I have not got a gun,
And if I had, your life's work would be finished and done.
The Good Lord created all things,
And most into my life some pleasure brings.
Except you, black bastard
With heart cruel and hard.
The devil claimed you for his own.
In your heart his corruption was sown.
It bore fruit, and now your foul deeds
Sicken my soul and make my heart bleed.
Lambs with eyes and tongues pecked out.
Eggs of nesting birds strewn about.
You do a little good, I'll say that
Tidying up corpses round about.
But other creatures do the same
And they don't play your other filthy games.
Go away, you demon, stop spoiling my day
Go back to the devil, that's what I say!

## The Hawk

I saw a hawk, soaring in the air,
Riding the thermals without a care.
Up with her my spirit did go,
Left all my cares down below.
I rode the wind, I was free,
Far from all human misery.
In the air peace did reign
Down below all stress and strain.
When troubles come and you feel under the weather
Think of the hawk,
And me,
And you'll feel better.

# The Robin

Wherever I am, one seeks me out,
I'm never alone, a robin is aye about.
Flame red breast burns so bright,
In the woods' gloomy winter light.
He inspects every single thing that I do
Felling trees, cleaning ditches, even before I'm through.
He's there beside me almost as soon as I've begun
Like a bossy wee gaffer who wants the job quickly done.
When piece time comes he's right in about,
What's in the bag today? He seems to shout!
Keeps me company all day long
With chivvying help and chirpy song.


# The Whooper Swans

I heard the whooper swans at last today,
I've missed their beautiful, mournful trumpeting cry,
Scanned the skies for weeks now,
Strained my ears and wished them to swoop down low.
But I've either been too busy, wrong time, wrong place,
Head bent low over the saw, noise and fumes in my face.
Today I heard, then saw them, by pure chance,
Coming in low, made my heart dance.
A big skein, flying low from the east.
How beautiful, entrancing, a sensual feast!
I was leaning out of a window, checking a roof that was leaking,
I heard them, forget the job, for the swans I was seeking.
Welcome back big birds, though you herald winter cold.
A sight like this is a joy to behold.

## Lapwings

I remember how, as a boy in south west Lancashire
You would congregate on the stubbles in large flocks in winter,
And as I watched your ariel tumblings,
I would marvel at your skill;
Flinging yourselves zig-zag across the sky,
Then hurtling towards the ground
And at the last moment, climbing skywards again.
Later, as a youth, when I toiled in the hills,
I knew your return heralded the return of spring
And an end to winter's iron grip upon the land.
I learnt other names for you Teachit, Peesie, Plover.
I moved your eggs gently aside, when harrowing spring tilth
And then moved them back again to your scrape in the ground.
You and Oyster Catchers would be my companions
On long spring days of toil.
Now, as a man, your numbers are less and less
And I am sad.
Drainage, pesticides, fewer stubbles
Bigger machines, less time.
So a man will grub your eggs into the ground
Instead of stopping.
More crows too,
 Black bandits who rob your nests
And leave you bereft.
You have been with me all my life
I pray you still will be,
When I am old.

48

# Mole Catching

The gentleman in the black velvet jacket
Is at work again.
Casting up mounds of earth
And spoiling the sward,
The lawns and flower beds too.
Plants disturbed, seedlings upset,
He really makes quite a mess.
And so I must reach for the traps
To do battle again
Against an unseen enemy.
Sometimes the contest is swift and quick,
Other times a war of attrition
As we try to outwit each other.
The elation I feel when I have secured victory
And his body lies inert in the trap
Swiftly turns to sorrow
This gentle creature deserves respect.
If only he would keep to the woods
We could live in peace.

# The Pony Path

The pony path through the trees
Is neglected now and in a sorry state
Out of use except by me
Superfluous to modern needs.
Now the Argo reigns supreme,
And the ponies are no more.
The Argo needs a man less,
No feed, no rubbing down at night
No catching or coaxing when in stubborn mood.
Hay, hoof pick and saddle,
Replaced by diesel, oil and spanners.
The pony path is still now.
Few know of its existence
Now it is in Commission hands,
It's neglect is sad to see.
Water spews onto it, drains are no more.
Bracken in summer grows tall
And blocks the way,
As do fallen trees.
A new high fence crosses its path.
You need to be a hardy soul to walk it now.
And yet it is worth the struggle.
It follows the burn, gurgling down from the hill
Rocks, pools and waterfalls
Birch and rowan clinging to steep slopes.
Many delights to see
But sadly, by few but me.

## The Bogman

I know a bogman who lives on Farr Estate,
Folk say he's horrible but he's my best mate.
Men shout at him, he makes the women scream,
Just because he's mucky and not very clean.
But I like him, and I'll tell you why.
Because underneath the muck
 He's really a nice guy.

## Bogged
*(The feelings of a man who has stuck his vehicle)*

Damn and blast, I'm stuck fast
Bogged down to the axles, right in deep
Why did I try to cross here?
I knew it was wet
Thought I could get out
And writhing to and fro, I've made it worse.
In full view of the road too.
The strath will have a good laugh at me.
Nowt for it. I'll have to walk
Down to the neighbours' for help.
He's got a big tractor, he'll get me out
After I've eaten humble pie
Being taken down now and then is no bad thing
Keeps your feet on the ground, teaches you humility
Stops you getting big-headed, and an insufferable bore.
So three cheers for the bog and its clarty wet mud

## Peat Cutting

Once there were many, now there are few
Cutting peats out here on the hill.
The whole district, old and young alike
Would once be out here, it was such a sight.
Friendships renewed, rivalries too
Love and jealousy, all the things folk do
Toiling away but now all gone
Only three left working under the sun
Which sometimes shines bright and burns us red
And sometimes it rains, and we're soaking wet
Sleet, even snow showers, roaring gales
And stinging our faces, the hammering hail.
 I've felt it all at the peats
But we work away, will not acknowledge defeat.
Today it is pleasant and a gentle breeze
Rustles the heather and the leaves
Of deer grass and down by the burn
The larch  needles dance and do a turn.
The curlew calls its sad lament
As we work away, our backs bent
To the toil and effort of securing winter heat
We work away at the peat

# At the Peats .......again!

It's two years now since I last cut peats in this bog
For I've other fuel to burn, plenty of logs.
But something drew me back into the heather,
To hack and toil, whatever the weather.
Freezing cold rain when I skinned the turf
It's a sore, hard fight winning fuel from the earth.
Cold, hard winds when we cast the peats
Though it was May, there was little heat.
This tradition will die with me when I leave this place.
The last peat cutter in Strathnairn, but I'll not break the faith,
With the last generation who grafted and worked
Year after year on the moss and never shirked.
Names, faces, some I knew but most I did not
Their prescence I feel as I cut my lot.
Some went off to fight in two world wars,
Never returned to Scotland's shores.
Or still farther back, to follow a Jacobite lad
To Culloden's calamity and a world gone mad.
The cold winds cry of grief, sorrow and fear
When I work up here, it's more than the cold that makes my eyes
fill with tears.
Though come summer warmth and I set the peats up in stooks
This moss takes on a far different look.
The breeze whisper of picnics, beer and laughter,
Of courting and love, and happy ever after.
If I stopped cutting peats, it would seem such a crime
Another tradition lost, condemned to the mists of time.

# The Peat Thief

*(Dedicated to all townies and tourists who have
helped themselves to "a few peats")*

This is the tale of a townie
Who stole a poor man's peats
Such a heinous crime, a despicable deed
It would make a strong man weep
"The peat costs nowt," the townie said,
"It's there lying free,"
She didn't see the work and graft
Of toiling hill-billies.
First the removing of heather sod,
tough roots to cut and hack
Then barrowing out top layers of peats
That gives you an aching back.
A second layer must then be cast,
Once more your back is bent.
By end of day, be it wet or fine
Your energy's all spent.
Even then the work's not done
For peats they must be stacked
Into wee stooks upon the turf
Once more an aching back
And then the day finally dawns,
We're off to cart them home
But someone else has been in first
Half the peats are gone!
I think there is no lower crime,
It makes my anger boil!
"The peats cost nothing," the townie said.
No, nowt but DAMN HARD TOIL!!

# The Peat Moss Laddie

Dave is a musician, he plays far and wide.
Travels the Highlands over, his guitar at his side.
He makes a reasonable living, but he aye likes something for free,
So he comes up to the peat moss to try and help me.

*Dave can play the guitar much better than me,*
*But when he's on the peat moss he's a sad sight to see.*

Dave helps at the peats, I'll give him credit for that,
Cos most folks these days, don't want to bend their backs.
The annual peat cutting is too much like hard work.
So I'll put up with Dave, at least he never shirks.

*Dave can play the guitar much better than me,*
*But when he's on the peat moss he's a sad sight to see*

I don't let him use the peat spades, they're family heirlooms.
He'd just bend and break them, he's a muckle clumsy loon.
The peat barrowing is in danger of becoming kindling sticks.
The number of times he's cowped it, it'll soon be in bits.

*Dave can play the guitar much better than me,*
*But when he's on the peat moss he's a sad sight to see.*

And when it comes to stooking , you've never seen such a sight.
Dave's heap falls over the very first night.
I have to go and rebuild them, it's a pain in the back.
If I could find someone else, I'd give Dave the sack.

*Dave can play the guitar much better than me,*
*But when he's on the peat moss he's a sad sight to see*

My wife shouldn't have let me buy this old guitar,
And Dave shouldn't have taught me the chords that
got me this far. They should have cut my tongue out,
and hacked off both my hands Cos then I wouldn't be
 bothering you with my stupid songs.

*Dave can play the guitar much better than me,*
*But when he's on the peat moss he's a sad sight to see*

# Alan's Lament

Alan's cold and lonely, sitting by an empty fire.
Cold and lonely, his fuel bills are getting higher.
Cold and lonely, staring at an empty grate.
Wishing he was Simon's fortieth best mate.
Alan can remember when he got free backs.
And when his yard was full of fire wood stacks.
Oh how he wishes he'd treated Simon right,
'Cos now he wouldn't be cold sod, Alan Speight,
Alan miscalled Simon, nearly all the time.
Full of negative vibes, he would whinge and whine.
Alan was a sneak, a rotten little clype,
Always running and telling tales to Simon's wife.

# Friendship

In this life you will have
Many acquaintances but perhaps few real friends.
True friends will not begrudge your good fortune,
Nor desert you when things go wrong.
True friends will keep a confidence.
They will laugh with you, share your joy and pain,
Like a member of your family.
They will worry for you in times of distress
And pray for you always.
A true friend is someone you can be at ease with,
In conversation or in silence.
A true friend will forgive you.
True friends can be of either sex,
Of any age, creed or colour
And I count you as one.

# The Nairn

By the river Nairn I pen these lines,
As the steady trickle of the water soothes my mind,
A dry spell, the river runs low,
But come the rains it will not be so;
Then it roars like a mighty bull,
tumbling, rolling with foam decked spew.
But now it is a gentle, peaceful day
For it is the middle of May.
Cuckoo and chaffinch sing in the trees
And violets quiver in a gentle breeze.
A sandpiper flies up river, scolding me
For daring to enter its territory.
I could sit here all day at my ease
But alas, work does intercede.
I take my leave, Farewell, Goodbye
To the river Nairn and its sweet lullaby.

## The Loch Seat

I walked past the loch one Sunday afternoon,
On a day that promised spring.
And there on the seat overlooking the loch,
Was a mother and baby, all happed against the chill.
The father was taking a photograph
It looked such a happy scene,
The mother smiled serene.
Behind, the loch stood glassy calm,
I smiled, waved and walked on.
Never spoke, did not want to disturb
Such a pleasant sight.
I did not know them,
Probably never will.
Joy, good health and happiness to them all!

# The Ruined Croft House

This wee hoosie has lain empty now for many a year.
But once it was a home.
The hearth is dead and bare
Where once there was warmth and flame.
To many it is nowt but an empty shell
But I feel a presence all too well.
Once, folk lived here laughed, wept, loved, argued and fought.
I can sense something of them here still.
Their hopes and fears I know full well
Good weather for seed time, lambing and hairst.
Dry weather for the peats and sticks
Not too long a winter, and good health too.
Though generations separate us we have much in common
And the craic between us would have been good
For we are all sons and daughters of the soil
Not like my neighbours now.
Now I feel isolated,
Marooned from a tide of life that is passing me by.
A relic, a fossil, a dinosaur
Belonging to another time, another place.
Few really know me
And even less understand
We are exhorted to embrace new technology
Yet I run pell mell from it
Am I and my way of life so wrong?

# The Fank

At the foot of the hill, up by the river
Lies the stone walled fank, unused now for many a year.
But each time I pass I think of the hard work
That went on there.
The tasks of the shepherds year
Of gatherings on the hill.
Dogs and masters sometimes working well,
And sometimes not.
Loud would be the cursings,
And Moss, Sweep and Nell would be damned to hell
But only for a while.
Hard work in itself the gathering,
But the real work began in the fank.
Shedding ewes from lambs,
Then according to the season,
Castrating, drenching, vaccinating,
Checking mouths and udders,
Trimming feet and dirty tails.
Worst of all, the dipping,
Hot, heavy, wet work
Soaked in sweat and dip alike.
Thrawn sheep, and who could blame them,
For I would not want to go into that stinking bath.
Yet it was for their own good,
To protect them from ticks, lice, blowfly,
Parasites that would literally devour them.
When the days work was done, back to the hill.
Dogs and shepherds tired,
This was the life of the fank

## Granite of Farr

Grey and cold, one of the hardest of stones
Great chunks lie on this strath floor, like huge, bare bones.
Harsh and unyielding, you do not split as well
As limestone or sandstone. You are as tough as hell.
I admire the masons who could cut you into blocks.
How long that must have taken, how many knocks
And blows of hammer and chisels of steel
As they hacked and hewed and made you yield.
Such regular blocks I seldom build with,
For field dykes, I must make do with what nature gives.
Rounded lumps, dense, abrasive, heavy
A day working with you extracts quite a levy
On my hands all chapped, bleeding and sore
And my arms, legs, back for mercy do roar.
My mind is numb, my brain it aches
For dyking with rounded lumps it fairly takes
More out of you , than working with flat, rectangular shapes
Of sandstone, limestone and slate which do drape
The fells and dales of Northern England.
But in this strath , all that is at hand
Is you grey granite and you
Are the best that I have and must make do.
I do not hate you, I love you real well
For a well built dyke makes my heart swell
With pride and respect, my heart does glow
Could a wire fence do that? I do not think so.

## Bothy Song

It was a cold winter's night and the weather was rough
And inside the bothy, the living was tough.
There was me and my collie and her name was Kim,
 and supper once more came out of a tin.
The joys of living in a bothy.
There was no central heating , just an old rayburn stove,
Load her up with dry logs and boy could she go.
Not long after we'd finished our cordon bleu tea
Me and the collie would be asleep on the old settee.
No double glazing, just old sash windows,
You always knew which way the wind blows.
The curtains would toss and dance in the breeze
And the carpets would lift up around your knees.
The bathroom was as vast as a football pitch
And as inviting as an icy cold ditch.
The cast iron bath could have held four sheep.
Bath nights would make a strong man weep.
Now this was no way to live your life
So I got hitched up with a wife.
Cuddles and hugs keep you warm and are fun.
And two in the bed is much better than one.

# To a Haggis

(*with apologies to R. Burns esq.*)
Blush with shame ye and your soncy face,
Great chieftain of the pudding race,
Fat, greasy, bainy slob.
I would not give ye a job.
Your high fat content has caused many a stroke,
And heart attacks, and made folk choke.
So against ye, I do rant and rage
There's no place for ye in this politically correct age.
Away with ye, ye sleekit beast
Make way for a healthy, high fibre feast

# A Love Song

Come away, my lassie, Come away with me,
To where the heather grows and the spirit can roam free.
Far from the city streets, to the hills above
Come away my lassie, Come and be my love.

When the winter breaks, and spring draws near,
The birdsong is loud, snowdrops do appear.
We can walk together, through the woods and glades.
Come away, my lassie, Do not be afraid.

When high summer is here, around mid July
When the sun beats down, from a cloudless sky
To the loch we'll go, and sit upon the shore.
Hand in hand my love, together evermore.

As the year grows old, and leaves turn golden brown
The stags start to roar, their cries echo around.
We'll walk arm in arm, under a moonlit sky.
Our love growing stronger, a love that'll never die

When the ground is white and winter stalks the land,
Lay aside all fear, I will take your hand.
Guide you through the snow, to the fireside
Come away, my love, Come and be my bride.

## Valentine

Wilt thou be my Valentine?
Wilt thou with me your heart entwine?
Wilt thou bless my lips with thine?
Wilt I be yours? As thou art mine

## Hugs

A hug is worth a thousand words,
It says I care, I sympathise, I love;
Healing the wounded soul
And soothing the broken heart
Going deeper, far deeper, than words ever can.

## Hurt

I can tell lass, that you've been hurt badly in the past,
Somebody, or something, has scarred you,
and still some pain lasts.
You smile more now but deep down there is still grief
And from it you haven't yet found total release.
But time passes by, and though healing comes slow
The river of hope and love will always flow.
You have friends and family who care for you deeply,
And will never desert you though life's path rises steeply.
Give us your hand, we'll help you to the top of this hill
From the summit of tomorrow, we'll help you through this ill.


## Beauty

Beauty is not seen in a face.
It lies hidden in a secret place.
True beauty is not complexion or unblemished
skin for it lies deep within.
It is kindness of thought, word and deed
To those around and, especially, those in need.
It is generous, forgiving, patient, kind
Found within the soul and the mind.
You can keep your society beauties, models and stars,
Give me a kind lady, one who cares.

# **To Margaret**

You took a rough and ready lad,
Firey- tempered, short- fused, selfish,
Moody, bloody- minded, and difficult
And forged me into something better.
Still, that work goes on.
We have had our shares of ups and downs,
More than enough.
I have not always been as attentive and kind,
As I should
But you stood by me with patience and kindness.
You worked on me.
I cannot put into words
How much I owe to you.
Except for this,
I love you.

# **Tourists**

The tourists in the camper van, going slowly down the road.
Ignoring all the passing places, never doing as they're told.
Frustration causes accidents and the locals have work to do.
For goodness sake pull over and admire the view!
Get out, get out, the flaming way
You're a liability and you'll cause a pile up today.
I'm going to modify my car and fit a machine gun
To blast caravans and camper vans away to kingdom come.
You are on holiday and have plenty of time,
We are still at work and have to meet deadlines.
The scenery is splendid and it looks better if you stop,
Instead of crawling along at a speed like hopscotch.
Don't get me wrong we like to see you here
Spending lots of money every single year,
Supporting tourism, creating lots of wealth.
But please consider our blood pressure and our health.

# Death

I met a stranger in a wood one cold January day
His eyes were troubled, his body stooped,
His face was sickly grey.
I took pity on this creature and stopped for a blether,
At first the chat was inconsequential,
I think we talked about the weather.
I opened up my bag and shared my piece with him
As we sat under a beech tree, upon a fallen limb.
I grew bold and asked him what troubled him so
And this is the answer he gave, a tale of grief and woe
"I am Death" he said "And it is my fate
To be a figure of fear that people so hate.
My brother, Life, is loved with wonder and awe,
I, on the other hand, are damned, cursed and more.
I didn't ask for this job, it fell to me by chance
And now for eternity I must perform my deadly dance.
It's not me that causes famine, poverty and war
It's not me that decides who'll be rich or who'll be poor.
In fact I do a service, I release folk from grief
From all pain and suffering, I give blessed relief.
And what lies for them in eternity,
It's not me that decides,
Heaven or Hell, purgatory or paradise
In their own hands it lies"
We sat for a while in silence,
Then we went our separate ways
I shook his hand and wished him well
As daylight began to fade
He smiled and said "Goodbye, my friend,
We'll meet again some day,
And when we do, have no fear
For my light will guide your way"

# Heaven

I cannot comprehend Heaven.
It is beyond the reach of my frail, earthly mind.
How can it hold billions of souls
And many more to come?
Infinity is too vast a subject for me
And omniscience and omnipresence of God too.
I cannot grasp, so I do not try.
Will there be gardens, woods, trees, dawn and night?
Will I be able to converse with the wise
Or laugh with fools?
Will my friends and loved ones be there?
Will there be parties, dances and praise?
I know not.
Will it be a journey
Or a rest?
Heaven, a word that excites, thrills and scares.
All I can do is trust in God
That he will find a place for me there.

## Leaving

If I should have to journey to a distant place,
And for a long time you would not see my face.
Think not unkindly of me,
Better to have happy memories
Of times we laughed, talked and gaily danced
Of soft smiles and a tender glance.
Forgive my impetuous, blundering rage
For I was more often a fool than a sage.
May you smile when you think of me
And , God willing, we'll meet in eternity.


## Changes

An old shepherd, long ago, once told me
"Changes and death, are in this life, the only certainties
Learn to accept them and go with the flow"
Wisely spoken but so hard to accept though.
Folk come into your life and then leave,
Some you never miss, and some you forever grieve.
Dear friends whose company you cherish depart,
Miles separate you and keep you too far apart.
Letters, phone calls and cards may be promised to be exchanged
But busy, hectic lives render our good intentions lame.
So here's to all dear friends and colleagues that I've met
Whose companionship and happy memories I treasure yet
Forgive my laziness, for not keeping in touch,
From the bottom of my heart I thank you so much.